Heart

Breathings

Other Books by Leonard Ravenhill

AMERICA IS TOO YOUNG TO DIE

MEAT FOR MEN

REVIVAL GOD'S WAY

REVIVAL PRAYING

SODOM HAD NO BIBLE

TRIED & TRANSFIGURED

WHY REVIVAL TARRIES

Heart

Breathings

by
Leonard Ravenhill

UNITED STATES ADDRESS
Harvey Christian Publishers, Inc.
449, Hackett Pike, Richmond, KY 40495
Tel./Fax (423) 768-2297
E-mail: books@harveycp.com
http://www.harveycp.com

BRITISH ADDRESS
Harvey Christian Publishers UK
11 Chapel Lane, Kingsley Holt
Stoke-on-Trent, ST10 2BG
Tel./Fax (01538) 756391
E-mail: jjcook@mac.com

Printed in USA
First Edition 1995
This Edition 2013

ISBN: 978-1-932774-49-8

Cover Design by
Isaac Samuel
faithgrafikdesigns@gmail.com

Printed by
Lightning Source
La Vergne, TN 37086

Foreword

"Heart Breathings" is a fitting title for a book where words are only the vessel that somehow endeavors to hold, and show forth, the breathings of the spirit that is not flesh. There is a frustration when yearnings beyond words find themselves clothed in the only medium that can cause them to be tangible to others. These poems are the roarings and sighings and longings of the inarticulate soul trying to create a substance through which to transmit its feelings to others.

To my father, religion was of the heart—the realm of the Spirit's quickening life. Other sources failed to satisfy, and produced within him a hurt, a scorn, a weariness. For him, the heart was supremely important, and he saw that the only source of ministry to the heart was the Spirit of God—all else is at enmity. All the limits that reason, or society, or human frailty would interpose, were to be attacked without mercy. Any failure in Christians to give their all in response to God came under the same attack.

The mind has its measures and gives itself to the object of its thoughts in the degree that corresponds to its reasoning. The heart has no measures; with the heart it is either "yes" or "no," and the object that calls forth a "yes" is worthy of everything. The object that elicits a "no" is worthy of nothing. It is here where many misunderstood my father—they could never see, with him, that in the spiritual realm everything that is man-generated is absolutely valueless. His life and ministry were a passionate protest against the religion of the twentieth century in which man has made his image of God, not graven in stone but rather graven in words, and then set this up saying, "This is your God, worship Him."

My father saw God as infinitely beyond man's endeavors to explain Him, infinitely beyond man's efforts to serve Him. He saw God as an eternal fire of Infinite Life and Infinite Holiness— to be known in the total surrender of ourselves. He saw God as bringing us into an awareness of His limitless world where His holiness and mercy meet in a glory that transforms all it touches. God was to be known not by the mind but by the heart. Read then these poems with the heart, and you will find that the mind will follow on behind.

Paul Ravenhill
March 1995

About the Author

Leonard Ravenhill was born in Leeds, England, in 1907. After training at Cliff College, he entered on a widespread evangelistic ministry in the British Isles and in the U. S. He has also written a number of books, one of which, *Why Revival Tarries,* has been translated into more than five languages.

Mr. Ravenhill spent his last years living in Lindale, Texas, from which he traveled throughout the country. His books and messages, with their insistent call for repentance and revival among Christians, have inspired and challenged many. Perhaps his greatest ministry in later years consisted in personal contact with hundreds of hungry souls who came to his home for blessing and encouragement, or called him on the telephone. He did our ministry a great service by recommending our books to many of these people. Mr. Ravenhill passed away on Nov. 27, 1994.

A. W. Tozer said of Mr. Ravenhill, "Toward Leonard Ravenhill it is impossible to be neutral. His acquaintances are divided pretty neatly into two classes, those who love and admire him out of all proportion and those who hate him with perfect hatred. And what is true of the man is sure to be true of his books. . . . The reader will either close its pages to seek a place of prayer or he will toss it away in anger, his heart closed to its warnings and appeals." It is our prayer that this posthumous edition of Leonard Ravenhill's poems and sentence sermons will find readers of the former class, with hearts open to the burning passion for Christ found in these pages.

Index: Poetry

A Talk at the Wellside 56

Amazing Grace 23

Call Back 28

Calvary's Tree 53

Christ the Borrower 40

Eternal Night 31

Gethsemane 21

He Knows the Way He Taketh 34

I am a Slave 62

I am Thy Captive, Lord 20

I Did the Will of God 61

I Kiss Thy Rod 18

I Walked Today 15

In Heathendom 43

In Thy storehouse 49

It is Hell in My Soul 16

Judgment 44

Jungle Girl 45

Let Me Drink Thy Cup 36

Lord, Don't Ask Me 58

Lord, Emancipate 46

Love Like Thine 14

Men of Blood 52

Nearer, Still Nearer 54

Index: Poetry Cont.

Oh, Wonder of Wonders 25
Our Lethargy 38
Our Status Quo 47
Point'd Preachin' 39
Pour Thyself through Me 11
Seeking Thee 42
Some Work—Some Shirk... 48
Stephen 17
The Calvary Track 24
The Heathen.. 50
The Heroic C. T. Studd 29
The Martyr's Crown 37
The Revival Song 55
The Sweet Love of Jesus 19
The Victor's Pathway 26
The Wise Men Worshiped Him 32
This I know 60
Thy Glory 12
Thy Glory and Thy Majesty 27
Thy Sweet Correction 19
To Please My God 22

Pour Thyself through Me

Spirit of the living God, pray Thy mind through me;
Nothing less than Spirit-power do I ask of Thee.
Purge me, urge me, guide me, hide me—
Spirit of the living God, pray Thy mind through me.

Power of the eternal God, flow Thy power through me;
Holy, Pentecostal power do I ask of Thee.
Lowly, holy, for Thy glory—
Power of the eternal God, flow Thy power through me.

Mercy of the living God, channel love through me;
Nothing less than Calvary love meets the need for me.
Love that's burning, love that's yearning—
Mercy of the living God, channel love through me.

Grace of God, eternal grace, reach the lost through me;
Tenderness for every race do I ask of Thee.
Love them, lift them, reach them, teach them—
Grace of God, eternal grace, reach the lost through me.

Life of God, eternal life, pour Thyself through me;
Nothing less than Thine own life do I ask of Thee.
Life compelling, life that's telling—
Life of God, eternal life, pour Thyself through me.

Thy Glory

When Thy Shekinah glory fell,
　　The priests stood still in awe;
Nor could the great Apostle tell
　　The glory that he saw
When Thou didst lift him to the sky
To sights unseen by mortal eye.

When Moses stood with unshod feet
　　And Thy great Presence felt,
No trumpeter could call retreat
　　While gazing where Thou dwelt!
He listened, raptured by Thy voice,
And strangely did his heart rejoice.

The toilers' fishing nets were left
　　In answer to Thy call,
And worldly men, of sense bereft
　　Before their feet would fall.
Those simple men Thou didst endue
With power original to You.

O Lord, we labor in a day
　　When men of faith are few,
Now just a remnant watch and pray.
　　Again we beg—endue
Thy church with apostolic power
For true revival in this hour.

Have we the holy channel blocked
    With unbelief and sin?
Have we not asked and sought and knocked
    To bring the glory in?
How is now Thy Spirit grieved
    That He withholds the shower
That would revival tide bring in
    And apostolic power?

Is Thy blest Holy Word unread?
    And have we ceased to pray?
Have carnal longings in our hearts
    Brought spiritual decay?
Come, great Physician, come,
    And circumcise the heart;
Fleshly impediments remove
    And all Thy might impart.

So let the beauty of the Lord
    On Christians be outpoured,
That we forget "our" ministry,
    And glorify the Lord.
We hate the boasting flesh
    Which often claims Thy name.
Descend, Oh Holy Ghost, descend
    With all Thy purging flame!

Love Like Thine

Love divine all love excelling,
Love divine all love compelling,
Love that counts all things but dross
In the light of Calvary's cross.
Love that loves unto the death,
Love that loves with every breath.
Love that knows His deepest pain,
Love that gives and gives again.
Love that burns with holy fire,
Love that prays in His desire,
Love that's deeper—love that's higher;
Love that serves and knows no cost,
Love to reach a world deceived and lost.

I Walked Today

I walked today as Dante walked
    In days of long ago;
I gasped through stench of this earth's hell,
    The air was filled with woe.
Men scarred with sin, in rags, ill shod,
    Their face blank in despair,
Their livid eyes burned into me—
I cried, "O Christ of Calvary,
    Waken Thy church to care."

I walked today where Christ would walk
    If He were here on earth;
The air was thick with discontent
    And dark with lack of mirth.
It seemed despair had carved each face,
    And greed and lust and vice
Like chains, had bound resentful men.
"And, Lord," I asked, "Oh when, Oh when
Will Thy dear church revive again
    To seek Thy power in prayer?"

I walked today mid cultured vice
    And, as I walked, I wept.
I thought, Lord, of Thy sacrifice,
    And how Thy church has crept
Along the road this past decade
    And slumbered in soft pews,
While millions in their sinful plight
Fall into hell's eternal night.
O Christ, in mercy purge our blight;
    Anoint Thy church to tell!

(Written after a visit to a drug area in a large city).

It is Hell, It is Hell in My Soul

No peace like a river attendeth my way,
   My sorrows like sea-billows roll.
This heart-breaking lot has just taught me to say,
   It is hell, it is hell in my soul.

My sin—O the grief of this guilt in my heart—
   My anguish, not part, but the whole,
All adds up to loss, and I bear it alone;
   It is hell, it is hell in my soul.

Now Satan can buffet, sore trials can come,
   When life is all out of control;
My conscience just burns, and dark memories haunt,
   It is hell, it is hell in my soul.

But, Lord, haste the day that will chase off this night,
   And scatter this doom from my soul.
With tears I repent, so, dear Lord, let me know
   There is hope and relief for my soul.

With great condemnation I fall at Thy cross,
   To confess, not in part, but the whole
Of a sin-blighted life, and to cry to be cleansed,
   And to plead, "Take control of my soul."
Only then can I joy and rejoice as I sing
   Now it's well, it is well with my soul.

Stephen

They spilled out from the upper room
Not cowering or clothed with gloom.
They were ablaze with holy fire,
Fully consumed with one desire—
To know and to be known by Him
Who purged them from defiling sin,
To let the Temple crowd just see
How holy simple man can be.

By God they formed a holy band
Who would, through Him, possess the land.
They formed a special holy crew,
—A deacon band, something quite new.
Men Christ saved to the uttermost;
Purged and filled with the Holy Ghost.
They heard from God that His first choice
Was one called Stephen, a faith-filled youth.

This flaming soul, with holy power,
Did wonders and miracles by the hour.
The other apostles, beaten and in jail,
Were not in fear—they just prevailed.
They could not be intimidated.
Why? Just because they were related
To One above upon a Throne
Who kept His touch upon His own.

The more men beat this holy crew
The more their testimony grew.
Never did men of any nation
Hear anywhere a greater oration
Than that which Bro. Stephen gave,
Choosing not <u>his</u> life to save.

Into an outer court thy led him,
Battered his body, stoned and bled him.
He saw that crowd through blooded eyes,
He further saw—into the skies,
And, surely to his great surprise,
He saw his Lord and Savior rise
Before the throne at God's right hand
To welcome him to his Homeland!

I Kiss Thy Rod

I bow my head, my Holy God,
To kiss Thy loving, chastening rod,
Because I know, how oft You smite,
It only can be true and right.
I want my simple life to be
A living copy, Lord, of Thee,
In love and Thy humility,
A humble, lowly, contrite heart
With truth set in the inward part.
Dear God, I really do aspire
For a soul inflamed with holy fire,
To burn with an untiring zeal.
O! Master! Master!! Let me feel
The inward throes of Your compassion
As my inner life You gently fashion,
Until men's eyes can see in me
Thy travail in Gethsemane.

The Sweet Love of Jesus

O, the sweet, sweet love of Jesus,
    Vaster, deeper than the sea,
Flowing in majestic fullness
    From His throne right down to me.
Love before me, love behind me,
    Love beneath and love above.
Love beyond man's full dimension,
Love beyond man's comprehension,
    Holy, awesome, endless love
Showered in mercy from His throne
Just for those He claims His own.

Thy Sweet Correction

How can I, Lord, repine
When I am surely Thine,
And, yet more wondrous still,
I know and do Thy will.
O Lord, what bliss is this
To know Thy soothing inward kiss!
To know Thee in a new dimension,
To welcome all Thy sweet correction,
And goads that lead me to perfection.
Thy rebukes are good for me,
They purge for deeper chastity,
They draw me closer to Thy breast,
And there, and only there, dear Lord, is perfect rest!

I Am Thy Captive, Lord

I am Thy captive, Lord,
   Not wishing to be free;
To know I am Thy bond-slave
   Is glorious liberty.
My life, my all, in Thy control,
Is glorious freedom to my soul.

I am not tossed about
   By vicious doctrine wind.
My soul is safely anchored
   Because I have Thy mind.
My will is Thine, Thy will is mine,
   And, in this my blest soul estate,
My longings do not wander far,
   I seek not to be great.

Just lead me in Thy garden, Lord,
The garden of Thy Holy Word.
It's loaded with a thousand spices—
Delicious fruits, boundless advices.
Lead on, O King, in full control,
Thou are the Master of my soul.

Gethsemane, Gethsemane

Gethsemane, Gethsemane,
Where Jesus groaned to set me free.
Way back there in eternity
He planned salvation full and free
For sinners such as you and me.

He felt hell's billows o'er Him roll;
They should have crushed my guilty soul.
He knew the ransom must be paid,
That on a cross He must be laid,
Deserted by His chosen few,
Deserted by His Father, too.

His depth of anguish who can tell
As He was buffeted by hell.
He had planned to die alone! Alone!
And turn that Cross into a Throne.
In pain He groaned for cruel hours,
Not for His own sins, but for ours.

The greatest purchase ever made
Was when His priceless blood was paid,
When sinless Jesus crucified
Gave up the ghost, in anguish died.
This caused a panic all through hell,
And every demon had to tell
That Satan suffered full defeat
And from that hour beat a retreat.

To see that on the Cross He laid
The everlasting ransom paid!
There on that dread Calvary
Death, sin and hell were crushed for me.
"It is finished," was His cry,
Death and hell had no reply!

In glorious majesty He rose
Triumphing over all His foes.
Angels chanted, "Here's the King,
"Ope the gates and let Him in."
King of glory! King of Peace!
Let Him give thy soul release.
Victory He now offers thee
For time and all eternity.

To Please My God

I ask no bliss
But this,
To know Thy will,
And it fulfill,
In every part
So that my heart,
Without alloy,
May know the joy
By peace
Or rod
To please
My God

Amazing Grace

Sin shall <u>not</u> have dominion over you.
This from God's Holy Word, and it is true,
   He forgives our sinful heart,
   Cleanses, purges every part.
   Takes sole possession of our throne
   Where sinful self has reigned alone.
   Drives out every foul desire,
   Cleanses with His holy fire!
   O, my soul, without alloy
   This on earth is Heavenly Joy.
   Daily I my vows will pay,
   Walking in the Holy Way.
   My will married to His will,
   Mine a life that He can fill
   With a love to reach the lost,
   Showing me what Calvary cost,
   Giving me anointed eyes
   That can see beyond the skies,
   Showing me His glorious Throne,
   Where, one day, we all shall stand
   And bow to kiss the <u>nail-pierced</u> Hand.
   Lord, blest Savior, can it be
   We'll share with Thee ETERNITY!
What bliss is this for us who once were so remiss!
                  AMAZING GRACE

The Calvary Track

They turned it into a circus,
    And the Actor writhed and fell.
They baptized Him with oaths and curses
    As He tried to save them from hell.
They burned with the fires of their pagan lust,
    He burned with a heart of love.
In the ragged road of a vassal king,
    He staggered beneath His load—
Not the chafing wood upon His back,
    But a greater, invisible load.
The angels wept at His bloody brow
    And the spittle upon His cheek;
They knew He could turn those men to stone,
    But He acted—Oh, so meek.
He fell in the dust—from which men came
    And from which He would lift them high;
And He carried a billion, billion sins
    As He staggered on to die.
He turned not back on that Calvary track
    With its grief and humiliation;
He had planned way back in eternity
    For us and for our salvation.
        Alone in dark Gethsemane—
        O Lord, how could it be?—
        He had to cry in agony,
        "Thy billows go over Me!"
He knew full well, it was black as hell,
    If God's will He consummated,
When for men like me, He went to that Tree—
    For souls He had created!

Oh, Wonder of Wonders!

Oh, wonder of wonders!
   My God, can it be
That Jesus has died
   For one rebel like me?
He lifted my bondage
   And soul's misery.
The Lord, King of Glory,
   Was wounded for me!

They led Him to trial;
   They spit in His face.
He bore it alone—
   Oh! Amazing His grace!
He bowed 'neath His burden,
   Was scourged in my place,
I'll sing it forever—
   "Amazing His Grace!"

With hands full of mercy,
   With heart full of good,
My spotless Redeemer
   Was nailed to the wood.
He suffered hell's torment
   My soul to set free,
Deserted by God
   As He hung on the tree.

He died, but He rose!
   He extracted death's sting!
He's living enthroned—
   My Savior, My King!

Let the earth hear His Voice,
  Men and angels proclaim:
"He's coming! He's coming!
  He's coming again!"

With the saints marching in,
  (I shall be in that throng!)
In the great "Hallelujahs,"
  (I'll join in that song!)
With apostles and prophets,
  But best, Lord, with Thee,
I shall live, I shall live,
  Eternally!

The Victor's Pathway

I could not live without Thee—
  My Lord, I would not try!
Earth has ten thousand pitfalls—
  I never would get by!
But, with Thy Holy Presence,
  Thy Promises inspire;
I tread the victor's pathway—
  Dear Lord, I'm climbing higher!

Thy Glory and Thy Majesty

Thy glory and Thy Majesty
Are seldom, Lord, revealed to me.
My sight is dim, my senses dumb,
I seldom dwell on "Kingdom come."
Men dwell among the things that rust,
We live in time—with all its dust.
I would my interests relocate,
And dwell on Thee, my God so great,
And contemplate Thy Majesty,
Concentrate on Thy Deity,
Thus cheat the thieving things of time,
Dwell on Thy Holiness sublime,
Thy matchless beauty fill my gaze,
And worship Thee through all my days!
And then—ah!—then, Eternity,
Boundless, unmarred felicity!
No more to sigh, only to sing
In rapturous praises to our King,
To gaze with rapture on His Face
And sing and sing Amazing Grace!

Call Back

If you are far ahead of me
    Along life's winding track,
If you have real supremacy
    As you carry your loaded pack,
If you have found some energy
    That lets you know no lack,
Friend, share your secret now with me—
    I ask you, please call back!

Some who went ahead of me
    Endured the thumbscrew and the rack.
In biting pain they felt it gain
    To endure and not turn back.
They were sawn asunder, torn in two,
    Their bodies were beaten black.
But they went the last mile with a song and a smile
    For the One Who turned not back!

Now let me tell of the living hell
    Some saints endure today;
To be tied in a sack or stretched on the rack
    Would seem an easier way.
But they die by the inch, and they do not flinch
    As they tread their prison track;
And they inwardly sing to Christ their King
    That they'll never, no never, turn back!

It's a steep, rough road that leads to God—
    We must climb its hill with a will
To carry our load on the toughest road,
    His purpose to fulfill.
There may be strain, there may be pain.
    And the food may seem "hard-tack";
But He made it plain, there's eternal gain
    For the one who turns not back!

The Heroic C. T. Studd

Old Charlie was a cricketer
    (As most of you will know);
And when he played the lordly game
    He always stole the show.
He "drove" and "pulled" and "pushed" and "cut"
    That ball with lots of ease;
And to bewildered bowlers
    Charlie was a tiresome tease.

But Charlie quit the game one day;
    He gave away his bat
With a "Hallelujah!" and a grin,
    And then hung up his hat.
The vision Charlie had received
    Made cricket look so minor
He gladly counted all things loss
    And sailed away to China.

For Charlie made "The Cambridge Seven"
    (Oh, what a regal crew!);
He said, "I'm going now, dear Lord,
    What wilt Thou have me to do?"
With Smith and Polhill and the rest
    He did a man-size task,
And tackled any ugly thing
    The Lord did ever ask.

When Charlie got to fifty-three,
    He sat and asked himself
If now his work was finished here
    And he left on the shelf.

But suddenly the challenge came,
And he, with heart aglow,
Set out to face a greater task
Locked in the dark Congo.

Dear Charlie was "a fool for Christ"
With never a lament,
And counted nothing sacrifice,
But gladly he was spent.
"If Jesus Christ be God," he said,
"And He has died for me,
"O shame to talk of suffering
In the light of Calvary."

Aye, Charlie loved and dared for God;
No man who lived was bolder.
Oh where's the man who'd ever dare
Call Studd a chocolate soldier?
In God alone he trusted,
And God a hero made,
And in him God prepared a womb
To birth a great Crusade!

In this hour of great declension
We wish the churches would
Furnish ten thousand heroes
With hearts aflame like Studd.
We'd roll back dark apostasy
In every land and nation,
And, through this mighty rescue shop,
Steal millions from damnation.

Eternal Night

Eternal night! Eternal night!
   How dark that night will be
For millions who've not had the light
But who had every human right
   To share that Light with me!

When we shall stand around Christ's throne,
   We'll surely be remiss
That they have never, never known
Salvation through His blood alone,
   What tragedy is this!

Oh, how shall I, whose present sphere
   Is to be cleansed and free,
Stand uncondemned before Thy throne
While millions die—in hell to groan
   For all eternity!

Arm of the Lord, awake, awake,
   Thy church cleanse and renew;
And sanctify, endue with power,
Then thrust her forth this very hour
   Thy perfect will to do.

The Wise Men Worshiped Him

You have ears to hear? Then come, draw near,
  And listen to my solo
On the greatest event heaven ever sent!
  (My version's via Marco Polo.)
"The three wise men were kings," says Marco,
  "In search of the King of Glory!"
And I, for one, am going to hear
  While he unfolds the story:

"Gaspar from hoary Tarshish came,
Erect of head, with ancient name;
He came through dangers; he came afar,
Held to his course by a guiding star.
His beast swayed under a burdened back
With the weight of the gifts and the young king black—
A young king, strong and straight as an arrow,
No fear in his heart or down to his marrow;
Strong, reckless, happy, thrilled, and bold,
He sought for the King and he brought royal gold.
He slept by day and moved by night
(For only then the star gave light);
Without the star he might miss the way
That led to the Lord of Eternal Day.
As the time sped on, he went faster, faster,
Fearing that death or some disaster
Would rob him of getting that lasting joy
His heart had craved since a little boy.
In the dangers of brigands and bears at night
He was warmed by the star and cheered by its light.

"A city he saw, and, drawing near,
Met Belthazar, king of famed Chaldee,
Whose feet the wearying miles had trod,
His soul athirst for the living God.

'That I might find Him,' was his humble cry
As he swept a tear from his wind-cut eye;
'For life without God does not make sense,'
He said as he clutched his frankincense.
And though he was king of famed Chaldee,
And though he had riches without a peer,
And though he could rule with an iron rod,
And though he could get his way with a nod,
And though men bowed and revered his name,
His heart was sinful—just the same
As the king's who had feasted at his table,
Or the boy's who had cleaned his unclean stable.
So he sought for the God Who could cleanse from sin
And end the curse and chaos within.
The two raced on, ignoring all views,
Or the innkeeper's warning and scaring news.
As they smoothly moved, without ever a word,
They conscious grew of the form of a third.
King Gaspar challenged: 'Your name, good Sire?'
And, trembling with age, he answered, 'Melchior—
'And I'm seeking the Gift of gifts most dear'
Though I'm lord and king of famed Nubia.
I seek the Redeemer, the Sufferer!
My humble gift?—just a gift of myrrh.'

"And now the kings (and they were three)
Moved on to the nativity.
The star led on where Mary sat,
Caroling her magnificat.
'My soul doth magnify . . .,' she sang,
Until the very stable rang.
They found their Savior, King, and Lord,
With gifts they worshiped and adored."

WISE men worshiped! They still do—
A lesson, friend, to me and you.

He Knows the Way He Taketh,
And I Will Walk With Him

God called to us, His people,
   To be His holy Bride.
From out the rest of living souls,
   He calls us to His side.

The way He calls is rugged, steep;
The way He knows—we are His sheep.
No blind design—He has the goals;
His love leads to the waterholes,
Gives us this day our daily bread,
And hitherto He's always led.
Though dark the way, though the path be steep,
He drives the wolves from us, His sheep.
At times the clouds obscure His face,
But, bless His name, supplies of Grace
Can fortify 'gainst every shock.
His wisdom plans for all the flock.
Just now the skies seem solid brass;
Fear not, just think: "It came—to <u>pass</u>!"
The furnace seven times hotter be,
"My Grace" sufficient is for thee.
   Your soul is riding out the gale;
   Your courage falters, and the tale
      Is not yet told,
      But brighter gold
Comes from this long hostility.
And Jesus says, "Look unto Me—
I've planned for thee eternal days,
I've planned for thee a thousand ways.
I went through MY Gethsemane,
Will YOU, my child, bear this for Me?
My back was stripped, I bore the rod,
Will you bear this for Me, your God?

I've planed for thee a jeweled crown,
Will you 'go through,' or let Me down?"
Can you bear up a few more years,
Or will you cause your Master tears?

While Joseph's brothers made a pile,
Young Joseph suffered for a while.
That "while" just seemed a lengthy season
With no design, no rhyme or reason.
The brothers didn't care a bit
That Joseph languished in a pit.
They showed no sorrow for his plight;
They cared not for the wrong or right,
BUT God was there behind the cloud!
(He does not shout His plans aloud).
The path through pit and prison led—
For Joseph—to the nation's head.
Not then did Joseph weep or groan,
Each step was leading to a throne!
The starving brothers soon behold
A ruler with a chain of gold.
They wept and each his breast did smite
Before one sold to th' Ishmaelite,
Their brother! With the power of death!
Each man fell down with panting breath.
Forgiving, Joseph understood:
"Ye meant me evil—God meant good!
He did not leave me or forsake.
He knew each step I had to take.
My Shepherd led by pastures green;
No other way could there have been
For ME to prove that He is God.
I loved the dark, I kissed the rod!"

Now through a darksome glass we see;
But OH! the GLORY yet to be!

Let me Drink Thy Cup

Prune my withered branch;
  Dung my fruitless tree;
Spring up my dried out well,
  O Christ of Calvary.

Touch my dimming eyes;
  Oil my stammering tongue;
Complete, dear Lord, in me
  What Thou hast scarce begun.

Power me for the load;
  Wean me for Thy will;
Love me with Thy rod,
  And more I'll love Thee still.

Of Thy suffering, Lord,
  I pray, "fill me up,"
That I may follow Thee.
  O let me drink Thy cup!

The Martyr's Crown

The saints of old were beaten, tried,
Condemned and even crucified.
These martyr men beat no retreat
When flames were licking at their feet.
They saw the tyrants' brandished steel,
But still they offered no appeal.
They struck no bargain for their lives,
For their children or their wives;
All slowly roasted in the flames
While angels wrote each of their names
Within a book God calls His own,
To be proclaimed before His throne.
Then we shall know of their renown
When each receives his martyr's crown,
When God shall say to them, "Well done—
You ran the race, pressed on, and won
When in that race men said 'Insane!'
But now I gladly own your name.
Now you are home—come dwell with Me
In joy through all eternity."

Our Lethargy

I walked down the steaming jungle path
  'Mid exotic flowers and trees,
There were streams and gorgeous butterflies,
  But my mind was not fixed on these.
My head and my feet were burning,
  But my heart burned hotter with shame
As I saw the diseased and degraded
  Who never had heard His name.

I thought of our stately churches
  And their softly cushioned pews,
And I wept for the sin-damned millions
  Who never had heard the News
Of the spotless Christ of Calvary
  Who died their souls to save.
Unless there's a change, that heathen mass
  Will go Christless to the grave.

God, pity our empty fullness;
  God, pity our barren tree;
God, pity our long-range blindness;
  God, curse our lethargy!
Turn our much-used words into action;
  Change ease into Spirit-born care;
Baptize us with Thy compassion
  That puts feet under our prayer.

Point'd Preachin'

My pastor's getting out of hand,
He asked me did I understand
That soon all men from every land
Before a holy God will stand.
He said, "Then you may tell the Lord
Why He should give you some reward."

But surely angels will remember,
I bought a chalice last September.
It was pure gold, that lovely chalice,
With money left by old Aunt Alice.
Can all my works be burned to cinders?
I also bought two stained-glass windows.

Don't pass my deeds up in a hurry,
They're spoken of through Wintonbury.
There's Jenny Jones and her old Sammy—
I paid their two weeks in Miami.
I've done a host of wondrous things—
Besides, we're not all rich as kings!

My pastor called my life a libel,
And said it was not like the Bible.
I can't read long (I need new glasses),
And get confused about Saul's asses—
And sure that story seems a boner
About a whale swallowed by Jonah.

I like religion hale and hearty—
A miss'n'ry film and ice cream party,
And pictures of the pyramids—
But we don't need those noisy kids;
They bring the worst side out of me.
Leave them at home—they have T. V.!
I pay my tithes and fill my pew—
Surely there's nothing else to do!

Christ the Borrower

God laid Him in a borrowed womb,
Men laid Him in a borrowed tomb;
   His life was borrow, borrow.

He had no pillow for His head,
A stone He borrowed then instead,
   He borrowed fish for dinner.
A cup He borrowed from a dame
Despite her rather sordid name,
   To help that thirsty sinner.

A borrowed boat from which to preach—
A borrowed mount on which to teach—
   No time for fun or leisure.
He borrowed once a lowly penny,
Since of His own He hadn't any,
   For each belonged to Caesar.

He rode upon a borrowed ass
That prophecy might come to pass,
   No horse or golden carriage,
A room He borrowed to celebrate
His last meal, and anticipate
   The supper of His marriage.

He borrowed (staggering to the mind)
The whole vast sin of humankind,
   Our sacrifice to be;
The Spotless One Who did such good
Was hammered to some borrowed wood
   With scarce an eye to pity.

His life was filled with "borrow, borrow,"
Acquainted with grief, this Man of Sorrow,
  Deserted by His friends.
They laid Him in a borrowed grave,
The Christ, the Mighty still to save—
  With death His "borrow" ends!

For soon, ah soon, the Victor rose
Triumphant over death and foes,
  All power and principality.
Who borrowed, borrows now no more,
Triumphant then and evermore,
  The Lord of all eternity.

He "was" before the world began—
This Son of God was Son of Man,
  But now he reigns forever.

Seeking Thee

Lord, I seek Thee for renewing
  Of my faith and of my love.
Rush and care are my undoing—
  Touch me, Savior, from above.

Chorus:
Seeking Thee, seeking Thee,
Touch and give me liberty.

Pass me not, O holy Savior,
  Leave me not to grope and fail.
Through Thy blood I seek Thy favor,
  With Thy grace I can prevail.

Faith moves in to claim the promise;
  Peace revives and floods my soul.
Make me now Thy chosen chalice,
  Giving drink that makes men whole.

In Heathendom

Millions are waiting yet
    In heathendom.
Will they the Gospel get
    In heathendom?
Who will arise and go
Out to this sin, this woe,
And Christ the Savior show
    To heathendom?

The sun will soon be set
    O'er heathendom.
But they are waiting yet
    In heathendom.
Lost in the fog of sin,
Will none these wanderers win
For Jesus Christ our King
From heathendom?

Will someone lead the way
    To heathendom?
Will others join the fray
    In heathendom?
Lord, raise a holy band
With hearts empowered to stand
All that you will demand
    For heathendom.

Judgment

Yes, east is east and west is west,
    But soon the twain shall meet,
For all roads north, east, west, and south
Shall join—with pleas from every mouth—
    At Christ's great Judgment Seat.

It staggers the mind—that ultimate day—
With earth's proud empires swept away,
When billions rise from their weary bones
To mix with kings of the oldest thrones
And share with them eternal groans.

All human values will alter then
At the greatest judgment known to men.
Who have nothing now, can have something then;
Who have something now, may have nothing when
We stand at the judgment beyond our ken.

God will view the kings and the conquerors
    Who ruled with pride over millions for years,
And wrote their own vain history
    In other men's blood and sweat and tears.
Rulers they'll be no longer then
    With terrible power as kings,
But naked they'll kneel at this judgment,
    Awaiting all that it brings.

For the angels kept a record.
    Unbiased the game was scored.
The angels patiently watched it
    Without a critical word.
But when the books are opened
    Before ten billion men,
And all is tried by God's blazing eye,
    Will the game be worth it then?

Jungle Girl

I looked in her eyes like saucers,
    Just a girl on the jungle track.
She was one of the forest's daughters
    With a bundle slung over her back.
She was naked except for a G-string,
    And as black as a cob of coal,
But the dirt on her smelly body
    Was white 'gainst the filth of her soul.

Beneath that skin was a woman,
    Though she looked as wild as a beast;
But she knew no rights as a woman,
    To say the very least.
She worked for her man in the daytime;
    She slaked his lust at night—
A woman, dear Lord, a woman
    Without her human right.

O Lord, as things are going,
    It very well might be
She'll learn of Communist Russia
    Before she learns of Thee.
I flick back a page of my memory
    To our churches and people there
Who spend less time a-praying
    Than they do in styling their hair;
Those who plan for frivolous parties
    With frolics and food and fun—
But no cares for the wasted hours
    With so little praying done.

O God, dear God, in compassion
    Look down on our tearless eye;
Baptize us with Thy Holy passion
    For the heathen we've left to die.

Lord, Emancipate

These doubts and fears for many years
   Have fettered up my soul.
Oh, blessed Lord, emancipate,
   Come now and take control!

I now aspire with strong desire
   To be a channel clean.
Oh, blessed Lord, emancipate,
   Reign where the "I" has been.

Oh, take me higher, endue with fire,
   Thy glory dwell within!
Oh, blessed Lord, emancipate
   And keep me free from sin!

Now free from sin, endue within;
   Give Thy compassion—tears;
Thou dost, my Lord, emancipate;
   Restore my wasted years.

At any loss I choose Thy cross;
   Earth's values I deplore.
Thy blood doth now emancipate;
   Thy victory I adore!

Our Status Quo

Oh, pastor, no, and again, no, no,
Do not disturb our status quo.
We love our Zion with cushioned ease
And ask you not to disturb us—please?
After all, we carry a little care,
And often sing "Sweet Hour of Prayer."
Dear pastor, we do not understand
Why you grieve for those in a foreign land.
We have the sick and needy poor
Ten yards outside of our own church door.
And, pastor dear, we often wonder
Why, at times, you seem to thunder
Against our hearts—which you say are cold—
(It seems to us you are very bold).
We believe in sin and regeneration;
Would you have us throw off the recreation
That gives us fun and makes us sleep?
Would you have us pray and fast and weep
For the heathen—lost, and, you say, damned?
(A thing we hardly understand.)
Our lives will need re-evaluation
If we are to care for another nation;
We have gorgeous homes, soft beds to die on;
We like it soft in our little Zion.
Oh, pastor, please again, no, no;
Do not disturb our status quo.

Some Work—Some Shirk

Some feast, some fast; some laugh, some groan;
　　Some fight their way to promotion.
Some labor and sweat almost unknown;
　　Some render unselfish devotion.

Some even boast of what <u>they</u> have done;
　　Some work with consecration;
Some speak only of Jesus the Son;
　　Some are full of self-adoration.

Some work with an eye on the glory;
　　Some work with an eye on the pay;
Some run with the Lord's blessed story;
　　Some work toward the Judgment Day.

Some tell of Thy great salvation;
　　Some bury their talent with care;
Some seek to evade tribulation;
　　Some know the soul-sweat in prayer.

Some doubt the power of Satan;
　　Some think they've "done all" and just stand;
Some shirk, with skill in evasion;
　　Some carry the burden He planned.

Some work for the night is coming;
　　Some toil in the heat of the day;
Some laze their hours just sunning;
　　Some fill their evenings with play.

Some will rejoice at the Judgment,
　　With deeds purified through the flame;
Some, with their works only ashes,
　　Will weep with regret for the shame.

In Thy Storehouse

There are riches in Thy storehouse,
    But, my Lord, we are so poor.
There is power in Thy storehouse,
    But the cripple clothes our door.
There is wisdom in Thy storehouse,
    But in ignorance we grope.
There's revival in Thy storehouse,
    But we've millions without hope.

There is freedom in Thy storehouse,
    But Thy people are so bound.
There is glory in Thy storehouse,
    But it does not shine around.
There is love within Thy storehouse,
    But Thy people are so dry.
There's compassion in Thy storehouse—
    Then my Savior, why, oh why
Are Thy people stony-hearted
    And our eyes so desert dry?

The Heathen

I'm gazing now in the jungle green
With a people whose bodies, not fit to be seen,
Are crusted with dirt and distorted in belly,
With louse-packed hair and revoltingly smelly.
A woman now swings her naked breast
To the mouth of a babe who was never dressed.

She sits in a house with mangy dogs
(The best of the room is reserved for hogs).
The husband knows nothing of horses or cows,
But boasts his wealth by his fertile sows.
The place is fit only for hogs and dogs
That snooze by the fire of smoldering logs.

I have seen them crouched in the desert heat;
I have heard the thud of their unshod feet.
I have seen them shake an unwashed head
As they cringed at the feet of their unsaved dead.
O God, it seems to be madly absurd
That they knew not Christ or Thy holy Word.

They have gone to hell while we slept in our pews;
While we argued doctrine, we denied them news.
We've reclined in plush and saved our knees;
We have had it lush and forgotten these
Who grope in fear in the heathen night.
Had we loved them once, we'd have sent them light.

O Christ, by the power of Thy holy Name,
Give Thy flabby Church a heart of shame.
Smite her cold conscience, buckle her knees,
That she has lacked concern for these
Who have, generation by generation,
Been lost to Thine own "so great salvation."

Oh God, on that day, that Judgment Day,
When homes and banks have been swept away,
And there is no place of habitation
For any man in any nation;
Then every man must stand alone
Before the King on His Judgment throne.

What shall I do when the heathen stand
And accuse that I seldom lent a hand
To save them from pain and eternal woe,
And stayed in my ease but made others go
With a message I knew, I knew full well
Could save them from sin and fear and hell?

O God, my God, in that dreadful day
When all excuses are tossed away
And there's no time left to repent or cry
As earthly treasures in ashes lie,
Then Lord, oh, Lord, what shall I say
For the money and time I have frittered away?

Men of Blood

There's a burden to be lifted,
And a barrier to be shifted
It would seem God's need is supermen today.
Wicked rulers in high places
Seem intent to ruin races,
While the Christians make their daisy chains and play.

God has need of soldiers true;
Demons laugh, recruits are few,
So that death and hell and Satan have their sway.
No! My son, the task's not done,
Scarcely has it yet begun;
Men—all classes—totter to the grave;
To that great eternal night,
With no ray of hope in sight,
Tramp lost millions whom our Jesus died to save.

Gracious God, our hearts inspire,
Touch us with celestial fire,
Give us burning heart, and bursting lips, and brimming eyes,
Strength of purpose, power of will,
There's a place for us to fill
And a victor's crown awaiting in the skies!

Calvary's Tree

I know that I shall never see
A tree like that on Calvary,
A tree on which men, poor and blind,
Defiled the Savior of mankind.
<u>That</u> sin was done by fools like me,
But God Himself was on that tree!

I love to think, as He hung there—
No eye to pity, none to care,
Victim of hate, betrayed and cursed,
Cut off from God, dying in thirst—
I love to think He thought of me
When hanging there upon the tree.

I joy to know He'll come again,
Who on a tree by man was slain.
I'll count myself among the wise
Who wait His coming from the skies;
Not from a tree, but from a throne
He soon shall rule this world alone.

(Dedicated to Gary Johnson)

Nearer, Still Nearer

Nearer, still nearer, I draw to Thee,
All through the offering that Thou gavest me.
Jesus my Savior, God's only Son,
Paid my redemption; now barriers are gone;
Paid my redemption; now barriers are gone.

Nearer, still nearer, Lord, I would come
All through the merits of Thine only Son;
His perfect offering cleanses my heart,
Now to this temple Thy Spirit impart;
Now to this temple Thy Spirit impart.

Nearer, still nearer; come more and more.
Jesus my Master, I long to adore
Thee for Thy mercy, patience and power;
Thee will I worship, rejoice evermore;
Thee will I worship, rejoice evermore.

Nearer, still nearer, down at Thy feet,
Through Thy atonement my offering's complete.
Sanctify body, spirit, and soul,
My all is utterly 'neath Thy control;
My all is utterly 'neath Thy control.

The Revival Song

(Tune: "There Shall be Showers")

Lord, we are hungry for blessing,
    This is in tune with Thy Word;
Now, as our need we're confessing,
    Give us new hearts, cleansed and stirred.

Chorus:
Visit our city,
    Lord, save our nation, we pray.
Quicken our love and our zeal, and
    Send us revival today!

Great is the need of our nations,
    Great is the need of this hour;
Lord, we abhor our stagnation,
    Answer with Holy Ghost power.

Look on our great desperation,
    Hold back Thy judgment we pray;
Move through the length of our nation,
    Open Thy windows today.

A Talk at the Wellside

She came to the well—'twas her custom,
   With waterpot, burden, and care;
Came at noonday so no one would see her,
   And found just a Stranger sat there.

He asked for a drink of well-water.
   (How deep her need only He knew!)
She asked, "Can a Samaritan woman
   Give drink to a thirsty young Jew?"

He said, "You should have living water
   That needeth no earthenware pot."
She gazed with wide-eyed amazement
   And wondered what secret He'd got.

She said, "Art Thou greater than Jacob,
   Our father, who gave us the well?"
She stayed, and she listened enraptured
   To all that the Stranger could tell.

He said, "Thou dost draw of this water,
   But comest again and again;
I can give thee the life-giving Water
   And in thee a well will remain!"

She answered, "Oh give me this water!"
    But hardly did she understand.
He said to the woman bewildered,
    "Away, and call thy husband."

She started this deep conversation
    And secretly wished she could stop it,
For now, to her great consternation,
    She found that this Man was a prophet.

Before, she had talked at the wellside
    And often enjoyed the short tryst;
But knew not on this great occasion
    She talked with the Savior, the Christ.

She said, "When Messias cometh,
    How wonderful He will be!
For He shall tell us of all things."
    He answered, "I, Woman, am He."

Away to the city to tell it,
    The news that could never be priced:
"Oh come, hear a Man Who knows all things!
    I found Him, and He is the Christ."

Lord, Don't Ask Me

I'm just a weak-kneed Christian,
    So, Lord, don't ask of me
That I go to the battle front
    To do exploits there for Thee.

I like to read of courage
    And Christians who make their mark;
But, Lord, that's surely not for me;
    I'm quiet and hate the dark!

I sometimes lie in bed at night,
    And it upsets my quiet
To think of heathen far away,
    Diseased and drunk in riot.

O Lord, a coward then I feel
    As in my bed I sink;
I'd like to sleep, forget it all,
    But I just think and think.

I muse on that great final day
    When at Thy throne I stand.
With flaming eyes You look at me
    And, under great duress,
I see excuses torn from me;
    I stand in nakedness

And hear You say, "You called me 'Lord,'
    And did not things I say.
You missed your glorious, great reward,
    You toyed your life away.

"You did not read and pray aright,
    Gave time to eat and drink,
And left the heathen far away
    To fall, fall right o'er the brink

"Of time, to hell's eternity
    To grope in endless night.
You could have stretched a hand to save,
    You could have changed that plight

"Less comfort had you had on earth,
    Then scores of precious souls
Had got the truth, and by your help
    Had reached God's offered goals."

From all my folly, Lord, I turn,
    I'll do as well as say;
And, from this hour, may all my works
    Survive the judgment day.

This I Know

Lord, I love Thee, this I know
For my conscience tells me so;
Sin I served for long, too long,
I was weak, but it was strong.

Chorus:

>Savior, I love Thee,
>Savior, I love Thee,
>Savior, I love Thee,
>And love to tell Thee so.

Lord, I love Thee and will stay
In this love-life all the way;
Jesus Savior is my song
In the night and all day long.

Lord, I love Thee, love Thee still
With my heart and soul and will;
Through Thy Cross I've perfect peace;
By Thy power have sweet release.

Lord, I love Thee for Thy grace,
And I long to see Thy face;
I will love Thee till I die,
Love Thee then for eons on high.

Lord, my love can only be
That Thou first hast loved me.
I love Thee much, I'd love Thee more;
All Thy love through me outpour.

I Did the Will of God

I fled Him when His grace pursued,
   I did despite unto His Name,
And delved me into sin so rude
   That there my soul enforged a chain.

When captive to my own desire,
   When blue with guilt and unnamed shame,
His long arm reached into the mire
   And plucked me out—blest be His Name!

Shall I leave others in their woe?
   Shall I ignore their cries who sink?
Forbid it, Lord; I'll rise and go
   'Twixt Thee and them to be a link.

Unwearied may I lift the load
   Of those who stagger 'neath sin's spell;
Stab my poor heart with love's strong goad
   To battle powers of earth and hell.

Earth's little strand is far too small
   To barter for the judgment day,
When powers and thrones and wealth and all
   Forever shall have passed away.

Oh, Day of days, when I shall be
   The cynosure of ten million eyes,
Oh, may my Savior say to me,
   "Well done," as my eternal prize.

When unsupported I shall stand
   Before Thy blazing bema seat,
Give me, my Lord, to understand,
   I did the will of God complete.

I Am a Slave

I am a slave! I have no will, no claim
    To property, to time or sleep.
I am a slave, and bear my Owner's Name!
    His ways are mine; with Him I joy or weep.

I am a slave! No tears are spent for ease,
    Nor do I freedom crave;
    I willing slave am I to follow to the grave
My Master. Bless His Name!

Strings for Your Harp

Outline

Part I. The Beginning
  A. The Savior 64
  B. The Bible 66

Part II. The Christian
  A. Salvation/Faith 68
  B. Spiritual Maturity 70

Part III. The Church
  A. The Bride of Christ 76
  B. The Persecuted Church 78
  C. The Evangelistic Church 79
  D. The Lukewarm Church 79
  E. The Leaders 83
    1. Overcomers 83
    2. Preachers 84
    3. The Prophets 86

Part IV. The Imperatives
  A. Prayer 89
  B. Revival 92
  C. Missions 96

Part V. The Conclusion
  A. The Second Coming 98
  B. The Judgment 100
  C. Eternity 101

Afterword 102

Strings for Your Harp

Part I. The Beginning

A. The Savior

God owed us nothing—He gave us everything pertaining to life and godliness in His Son, the Lord Jesus Christ.

No intelligent man has to be convinced that there is a God, though he may have to be convinced of which is the true God.

It was through a tree that the first Adam lost his purity and power.
It was on a tree that the last Adam bought back that purity and power for all who will accept Him.

Satan lied to man about God,
but he cannot lie to God about man.

The first Adam had a perfect environment,
but he failed.
The last Adam had a polluted environment,
but He triumphed!

God, Who made the first Adam without a mother, and Who made the last Adam without a father,
can easily make a saint out of a sinner.

Wise men came and worshiped Him. They still do.

God needs no alibis.

God needs no sponsors.

No man ever did, or ever will do God a favor—
God does all the favors.

A teacher may communicate truth by word.
It is taught only by example.

In a world suffocating in false love,
Divine love is like a breath of oxygen.

Jesus did not have the "Midas Touch,"
He had the Mercy Touch.

I find it most intriguing to contemplate the fact that while men are considering what place to give Jesus Christ in history, He has already decided what place to give them in eternity.

Are the things we are living for worth Christ's dying for?

Good Friday.
    Today—The Holy One
    The Lowly One
    The Only One—Died
To reconcile us to God—Amazing Grace!

How sad He must have been that mighty morning when He had shattered the powers of hell, when He had led captivity captive and given gifts unto men, to find as He emerged from the tomb, with a million demons behind Him mourning that mighty Resurrection, that there was no welcoming party for Him.

There can be no leadership of Christ without
the Lordship of Christ.

B. The Bible

The Bible is never wrong!
God does not have to retract, revise, repair, or recall one
word He has ever spoken.

Men give advice;
God gives guidance.

We have substituted "the Bible says"
for what the Bible does.

The only people who want to change the Gospel are those
who are unchanged by it.

If men would read their Bibles more,
they would need to read us writers less.

The power, the prayer, the pattern, and the progress of the
New Testament Church make electrifying reading!

The Bible—
It cannot be solved or dissolved by human power.
It was not put together by the human mind and cannot be
solved by it.
It was not put together by human hands and cannot be
destroyed by them.

Based on the Ten Commandments, any nation can progress.
Without those commandments, no nation can retain its soul.

Biblical prophecy is history written beforehand.

Ponder what the "Heroes of Faith" did without a Bible!
(Heb. 11).
Consider how little we do having the full Revelation of Divine Truth.

Interpreters of the book of "The Acts of the Apostles" seem to be intimidated by two possibilities:
1. The fear of being clubbed by criticism, or
2. The fear of being ostracized for fanaticism.

The Bible is not just a series of puzzles to be deciphered;
It is a chain of commandments to be obeyed.

Five minutes of Divine revelation
might be more illuminating
than five years of Bible school instruction.

We have a lovely, lively, liberating Gospel!

Part II. The Christian

A. Salvation/Faith

The greatest miracle that God can do today is to take an unholy man out of an unholy world and make him holy, then put him back into that unholy world and keep him holy in it.

It is nothing to plant a man on the moon compared with getting the Son <u>into</u> a man.

Faith needs no crutches.

If "Christ liveth in me" then I shall be very careful where I take Him.

It cost Jesus Christ everything to obtain eternal redemption for us.
It will cost us everything to obtain and maintain that redemption.

Faith is either dead earnest or just dead.

God will not penalize me for Adam's sin.
God will not penalize Adam for my sin.
But He will penalize each of us for our own sin.

God cannot be explained—
He can be experienced.

The Holy Spirit cannot be intimidated.
He came in tongues of Living Flame to teach, convince, subdue.

Our claim on the Lord is from our weakness
not from our strength,
from our poverty not from our riches,
from our ignorance not from our wisdom,
from our humility not from our superiority.

God will test the faith He is going to trust.

If faith were more vigorous it would be more victorious. (1
John 5:4).

No vice, however horrendous, will keep us out of Heaven if
repented of.
No virtue, however admirable, will get us into Heaven
without the blood of Christ.

"Faith" takes the guesswork out of tomorrow.
It confidently boasts, "My times are in Thy hands."

An experience with God cannot be shared;
it can only be described.

Sinners need cold comfort and hot preaching until they come
to a place of repentance.

I would rather be Balaam's ass for God
than the swiftest horse in Jehu's chariot.

God grant us perception from Heaven
to save us from deception on earth.

God has to work <u>in</u> a man
before He can work through a man.

To know <u>about</u> Christ is education.
To know <u>HIM</u> is emancipation.

B. Spiritual Maturity

Spiritual maturity comes not by book knowledge but by strict compliance to the revealed will of God.

I believe in instant purity for the believer,
but I do not believe in instant maturity by God in Grace.
Cleansing is immediate—by the Blood.
Conformity is progressive—by the rod!

Through the atoning death of Christ, heart purity is instant—
but progress is constant.

The law of spiritual progress goes like this:
    process then crisis,
    followed by a process then crisis,
    ad infinitum.

There is a "deeper life."
It is as deep as a personal Gethsemane
and as costly as a personal Calvary.

We are, each of us, as spiritual as we want to be.
The throttle is in our own hands.

Too many of us want to make a peace treaty with Christ, but will not make a total surrender to Christ.

A secret of victory:
    To do *what* God wants me to do;
    To do it *as* He wants it to be done;
    To do it *when* He wants it done.

There may be no more theological frontiers to explore,
but there are new dimensions of spirituality to explore—
new possibilities of Grace!

The Christian has every right to tell God he wants to be a
saint, but the Christian has no right to tell God how to make
him one.

It is much easier to wear a cross
than to bear a cross.

Whom the Lord loveth, He correcteth.
Correction is criticism in action.

Sanctification is not isolation (Simon Stylite's style), but
rather constant, Spirit-operated purification in a world of
militant corruption.

Knowledge is not character, but character is developed from
knowledge and obedience.

Lord, let nothing live in me that should die and let nothing
die in me that should live.

The worst thing that God gives us is better than the best
thing Satan offers.

No fruit is better than its tree.

I do not know the weather ahead,
I do know the path that I must tread.

Truth can be a mental idol until it gets into the "blood stream."
It then becomes a motivating force.

The Beatitudes should really "be"
attitudes of the Christian's life.

The Beatitudes should "be"
attitudes in our daily walk with God.

Cultivate cheerfulness.

Every mother is a career woman.

"He anointeth my head with oil."
If <u>He</u> does not anoint it, no one else can.

"He anointeth my head with oil."
Without the anointing, what use is a bishop's miter?

The self-centered suffer when others disappoint them.
The Christ-centered suffer when they disappoint others.

Better to have a hard will and a soft heart,
than to have a soft will and a hard heart.

We do not learn a thing merely by committing it to memory.
We learn solely by experiencing it.

Christ has not conquered my affections if He has to compete
for my attention.

Cleverness will enable a man to make a sermon.
Only compassion will make him a soul-winner.

The Christian who has the smile of God needs no status
symbols.

Who we are, whom we know, and what we know does not
interest the world. What we are and what we do does.

Children are afraid to walk in the dark.
Adults are afraid to walk in the Light.

A statement does not have to be profound to be important.

"To obey is better than sacrifice," but not an escape from it.

The infant Christian prays, "Bless me."
The mature Christian prays, "Make a blessing."

It seems that we have substituted contributions to God for sacrifice for Him.

What possessions a man has are not too important.
What possesses a man is.
Positions and possessions become obstructions to spiritual expansion when we set our affections on them.

One way to live the Christian life is to be sure you don't live it as other people do.

The pursuit of holiness must outreach all our other desires.

I refuse to let men flatter me or flatten me.

It is God Who worketh in us so that we may work out our own salvation.

The world is unimpressed with a man who has all his "dispensations" correct but his disposition all wrong.

"Tears" are a ministry untaught, unsought and unteachable.

"Think twice before you speak once."
Think three times, and you may not speak at all.

The Christian must say "no" to the whole world system which is but damnation frosted with the glitter of success and illuminated with scientific luster. He remembers that it is worm-eaten with depravity and has God's sentence of death upon it.

The Christian life is more than emotion,
but it is not without emotion.

There is a cost in discipleship—
God has no basement-bargain blessings.

You cannot draw a straight line with a crooked ruler.

Truth fears no exposure.

"The Baptism" is not an event, but an advent.

God asks the best we have
because He gave the Best He had.

We can give God much: our problems, our griefs, our praises—but we cannot give Him advice.

May we grow old slowly.
May we grow wise quickly.

The man God uses is the man the world, and often the church, abuses.

The Christian life is not always exciting,
but it is always exacting.

Meekness is often anger purified of self-interest.

I don't mind being "the least of all saints,"
but I don't want to be the most stupid of them.

If a million people smiled on me while I knew God frowned on me, I would not be happy. But if God smiled on me while a million people frowned on me, I would not be unhappy.

I cannot live on excitement—not even Christian excitement. I can live on inspiration—Spirit-born within me.

Our problem is stewardship, not leadership.

"Is this vile world a friend to Grace?" asks a poet. The answer is "no"—"sonship" today means hardship.

When folk seek my advice, I am a counselor.
When I give my advice, I'm meddling.

If Christ is not worth everything you have,
He is not worth anything you have.

He who gave all He had for me
demands that I give all I have to Him.

I would rather be disappointed than a disappointment.

A contentious spirit is a sign of immaturity.

Happiness is the goal of the sinner.
Holiness is the goal of the believer.

If we are seated with Him in the Heavenlies,
we'll not be sinning with them in the earthlies.

When Jesus laid aside His glory and took our flesh,
He knew it.
When we lay aside the flesh and walk in the Spirit,
we know it.

The sparrow hath found a house, but eagles dwell in lofty mountain grandeurs. Where do we live?

Part III. The Church

A. The Bride of Christ

The only imperishable thing on this earth is the Church of
the living God.
Stand up and cheer!

A holy God in a holy place
demands worship from a holy people.

It seems to me that we can get back to Apostolic Christianity
if we want to; or is:
>   the road too steep
>   the reproach too great
>   the price too high
>   the sacrifice too involved
>   and the stigma too unbearable to get up the hill of blessing?

Save us, Lord, from:
>   Misapplied Energy
>   Misused Money
>   Misdirected Effort

"We are compassed about with so great a cloud of witnesses,"
and witnessed about with so great a crowd of promises!

When did you or I last tip-toe out of the sanctuary saying,
"Surely God is in this place"?

In the darkness He holds my hand (Isa. 41:13); therefore, I
can stand and withstand even when I cannot understand.

There is no New Testament evidence that people in those days went to church to get saved. They went to church because they were saved—through the power of the testimony of Spirit-inflamed witnesses.

Apologetics for Christianity are one thing—reasonable; apologies for Christianity, something else—insufferable.

Preaching is proclaiming the Word of God.
Teaching is explaining it.

Revival is an explosion in the Church.
Evangelism is an expression of the Church.

What kind of a church would my church be
If all its members were just like me?

Like a lily on a polluted pond,
the Christian is to display God-likeness
in a world hostile to virtue and holiness.

If we abide in Him, we shall abound in Him.

"The wise man built his house upon the Rock," but notice
that he went through the storm also.
The difference was in the foundation, not in the storm.

God is not interested in making straw men;
He is interested in making strong men.

The Christian life is not a party but a pilgrimage.

We need a mighty, cleansing revival in the Church to prepare
the way of the Lord.

What is missing from our churches?
To use an Old Testament term, it is the burden of the Lord.

The burden of the Lord in the Old Testament was not for the Amalekites, Hittites, Perizzites or Jebusites; God's chief concern was Israel. In the same way, not a single epistle in the New Testament was addressed to the lost; every letter was addressed to Christians!

We have taught Christians to witness and to work,
but we have not taught them to worship.

What, then is the burden of the Lord for today?
He is concerned for sinners who are rebels, who have their fist up against God.
He is concerned for preachers, that they should preach His judgment.
And He is concerned for His Church, the Bride for whom He is coming.
He longs to baptize His blood-bought church with a baptism of fire and power—that the world might know!

The gates of hell will not prevail against the living Church of the living, exalted Christ. "I will build my church."
He can do it, He is doing it, and He will continue to do it.

B. The Persecuted Church

The power of His resurrection is sought.
The fellowship of His suffering is shirked.

Better to die doing something for God
than live to do nothing for Him.

C. The Evangelistic Church

In Acts 27 Paul was the insurance policy for all on board.

We have been spiritually satisfied with so little for so long, when there is so much land for us to possess!

O for a thousand tongues to speak of Him;
O for a thousand hearts to love Him;
O for a thousand minds to think of Him;
O for a thousand wills to surrender to Him;
O for a thousand lives to serve Him.

It is not always easy to do God's will,
but it is always possible.

Mercy is love in action.

Believers should not need to be corralled in a church building once a week to be stirred on behalf of lost men.

Millions of dollars have been raised "for missions" because the preachers have said that the last great commandment of Jesus to the Church was, "Go ye into all the world and preach the Gospel."
NOT SO! The first and the last great word of Christ to His Church was, "REPENT" (Matt. 4:17; Rev. 2:5; Rev. 3:19)!

D. The Lukewarm Church

Instead of the Church penetrating the provinces of materialism, materialism has punctured the power of the Church.

Beware of an unholy attitude towards holy things.

Criticism is one thing at least which we feel, "it is more blessed to give than to receive."

We talk Apostolic doctrine
 but lack Apostolic deeds.
We claim Apostolic faith
 but lack Apostolic fruit.
Some trumpet Apostolic power
 but lack Apostolic poverty.
Some claim Apostolic enduement
 but lack Apostolic accomplishment.
We may have Apostolic vocabularies.
 Do we have Apostolic victories?
Many claim Apostolic succession.
 Few, if any, dare claim Apostolic success!

In the past the Church has had too little of the mighty stuff,
and therefore too much of the wrong stuff,
to move the world for God.

Many present-day "Christians" are:
 hazy in their convictions,
 lazy in their commitments,
 and crazy if they think God will endure this torpor
 much longer.

I am constantly amazed that so many "well-rounded" persons are so edgy.

The Church used to be a lifeboat rescuing the perishing.
Now she is a cruise ship recruiting the promising.

If we have not too many men studying church history,
we have too few making it.

Our present "Christianity" sputters along on the two cylinders of tithing and <u>token</u> commitment instead of speeding along on the eight cylinders of <u>total</u> commitment.

This is a day of healthy unbelief and of sick faith.

A high steeple is useless if the pew-dwellers beneath it are walking low.

In this age of arrogant science, the Church does not need to bow its head in shame, but rather to bow its knees in repentance for its apathy.

I am embarrassed to be part of a church
that is an embarrassment to God.

If you dope the dog, why complain when it does not bark?

One can ride the current charismatic circuit today without any Biblical integrity or theological allegiance.

There is more truth muttered than uttered.

Jealously is love gone sour.

I am distressed at the zeal of the heretics and the amnesia of the believers.

If God had a "School of Failure," most of us would have graduated with honors—but He is merciful.

How little it takes to make us laugh.
How much it takes to make us weep.

Folk are more concerned about the hardening of their arteries than about the hardening of their hearts.

I am more afraid of sorcerers than of flying saucers.

"Property" sells best today on Easy Street.

There is a lot of foot-dragging in the area of obedience.

There is a roar of opposition to pollution in ecology,
but only a squeak of opposition to pollution in theology.

The world has lost the power to blush over its vice;
the Church has lost the power to weep over it.

The Church has many organizers,
   but few agonizers;
   many players and payers, but few pray-ers;
   many singers, but few clingers;
   lots of pastors, but few wrestlers;
   many fears, but few tears;
   much fashion, but little passion;
   many interferers, but few intercessors;
   many writers, but few fighters.

The trouble, as I see it, with the <u>present</u> interpretation of the promise in Acts 1:8, "Ye shall receive power," is that
   It is all sugar and no salt,
   all daylight and no darkness,
   all pleasure and no prisons,
   all privileges and no privations,
   all feastings and no fastings.

When we have raked over the whole muckheap of this decaying civilization, <u>my greatest grief is to see a sick Church in a dying world.</u>

We have never had a period when Bible knowledge was more extensive than today. We drown in a sea of interpretations. We are surfeited with millions of cassettes, books, seminars, Bible schools, seminaries, radio and TV sermons and lectures, but where, oh, where is Apostolic power, Apostolic purity, and Apostolic piety?

The One with eyes as a flame of fire saw through all the show of the Laodiceans. He sees through all our showmanship also. Joel says we are to sound an alarm in all God's holy mountain. Now is the time to do it. Christ was nauseated and disgusted with a church that bore His Name but not His nature. The church which flattered itself because of its commercial and political prowess was rejected in His sight. On the law of averages, God's house today is neither a house of prayer nor a house of power. As with Laodicea, so with us—He stands outside.

E. The Leaders

1. Overcomers

The explanation for the Christians' overcoming life in Christ is:

    a. Their covering (Rev. 12:11), "the blood of the Lamb."
    b. Their conviction, "the word of their testimony.
    c. Their covenant, "They loved not their lives unto the death."

The reward for this overcoming is:
- a. Rev. 2:7, "to eat of the tree of life."
- b. Rev. 2:11, "shall not be hurt of the second death."
- c. Rev. 2:17, "to eat of the hidden manna."
- d. Rev. 2:26, "to him will I give power over the nations."
- e. Rev. 2:28, "I will give him the morning star."
- f. Rev. 3:5, "the same shall be clothed in white raiment."
- g. Rev. 3:12, "Him . . . will I make a pillar in the temple of my God."
- h. Rev. 3:21, "To him that overcometh will I grant to sit with me in my throne." That's the ultimate reward and glory.

You may give a man an office in the church,
but you cannot give him authority—nor can you withhold it.
Divine authority is divinely given.

Romans 8:37, "more than conquerors," is an exclamation
of jubilation for the soul's emancipation!

2. Preachers

A preacher is man with a message from another world
to people in this world
who are going to that other world.

The successful preacher does not end his sermon with the congregation on its feet applauding <u>him;</u> but rather, he leaves it on its knees adoring <u>Him.</u>

Our preachers must be filled with the Spirit before they fill our pulpits, or else they will fill the people with chaff.

The message of the preacher is not always scathing,
but it is always searching—if it is Spirit-energized.

The effective preacher is the man who trembles at His Word, but who stands untremblingly to deliver that Word.

The preacher must taste the powers of another world, if he would preach to men of this world who are blind and deaf to the claims of the next world.

We have an abundance of "men of the cloth";
few—too few—men with sackcloth.

Wet-eyed preachers never deliver dry sermons.

A preacher cannot get "off the ground" until he prays, and he cannot keep on the ground after he prays—
his preaching will soar!

The petty Peter of pre-Pentecost days
became the prophet-preacher
of post-Pentecost days.

There is much more to preaching than merely being loaded with theological savvy and elastic vocabulary.

The pastor's task is to feed the flock, not to produce it.

Giving a man an "R-E-V" does not sanctify him any more than giving him a Ph. D. can edify him.

I am tired of preachers who act like lions in the pulpit, but play like kittens outside of it.

Some preachers spend so much time walking theological picket lines that they never enter the areas of true worship.

An evangelist with his eye on the "jackpot"
should be afraid of being labeled a "crackpot."

Pity him and pray for him—
the preacher who can mouth eternal truths to eternal souls
without pain, or tears, or burden.

3. The Prophets

The prophet in his day is fully accepted of God
and totally rejected by men.

In a day of faceless politicians and voiceless preachers,
there is not a more urgent national need than that we cry to
God for a prophet!

The prophet is God's detective seeking for lost spiritual
treasures. The degree of his effectiveness is determined by
the measure of his unpopularity.
Compromise is not known to him.
He has no price tags.
He is totally "otherworldly."
He is unquestionably controversial
and unpardonably hostile.
He marches to another drummer!
He breathes the rarefied air of inspiration.
He is a "seer" who comes to lead the blind.
He lives in the heights with God and comes
into the valley with a "Thus saith the Lord."
He shares some of the foreknowledge of God,
and so is aware of impending judgment.
He lives "in splendid isolation."
He is forthright and outright,
but he claims no birthright.
His message is, "Repent, be reconciled to God,
Or else. . . .!"
His prophecies are parried.
His truth brings torment,
but his voice is never void.

He is the villain of today
and the hero of tomorrow.
He is excommunicated while alive
and exalted when dead!
He is dishonored with epithets when breathing
and honored with epitaphs when dead.
He is a schoolmaster to bring us to Christ, but
few "make the grade" in his class.
He is friendless while living
and famous when dead.
He is against the "establishment" in ministry—
then established as a "saint" by posterity.
Daily he eats the bread of affliction while he ministers,
but he feeds the Bread of life to those who listen.
He walks before men for days,
but has walked before God for years.
He is a scourge to the nation
before he is scourged by the nation.
He announces, pronounces, and denounces!
He has a heart like a volcano
and his words are as fire.
The prophet is violated during his ministry,
but he is vindicated by history.

There is a terrible vacuum in Evangelical Christianity today.
The missing person in our ranks is the prophet.
The man with a terrible earnestness.
The man totally other-worldly.
The man rejected by other men,
even other good men,
because they consider him too austere,
too severely committed,
too negative and unsociable.

GOD'S MEN ARE IN HIDING UNTIL THE DAY
OF THEIR SHOWING FORTH. They will come.

Let him be as plain as John the Baptist.
Let him for a season be a voice crying in the wilderness of
modern theology and stagnant churchianity.
Let him be as selfless as Paul the apostle.
Let him, too, say and live, "This ONE thing I do."
Let him reject ecclesiastical favors.
Let him be self-abasing, non-self-seeking, non-self-projecting,
non-self-righteous, non-self-glorying, non-self-promoting.
Let him say nothing that will draw men to himself,
but only that which will move men to God.
Let him come daily from the throne-room of a holy God,
the place where he has received the order of the day.
Let him, under God, unstop the ears of the millions who are
deaf through the clatter of shekels milked from this hour of
material mesmerism.

Let him cry with a voice this century has not heard because
he has seen a vision no man in this century has seen.
God send us this Moses to lead us from the wilderness of
crass materialism, where the rattlesnakes of lust bite us and
where enlightened men, totally blind spiritually, lead us to
an ever-nearing Armageddon.

God have mercy; send us PROPHETS!

Part IV. The Imperatives

A. Prayer

The need of the Church today is for spiritual millionaires who can bring down the wealth of the world above on this stricken church age.

It is my solemn conviction that the Lord put the Church to groan in this groaning creation (Rom. 8:26) that she might reach millions who would otherwise groan for eons in a devil's hell.

Are we (who still have coals of fire on our altars) measuring ourselves by the fireless altars of neighboring churches instead of checking on the praying blaze of our saintly forebears?

THE NAME OF CHRIST
If we today could rediscover
The virtue in that Name,
The victory in that Name,
The violence in that Name,
We could set this world alight for God.

A sermon born in the head reaches the head;
a sermon born in the heart reaches the heart.

No Christian is greater than his prayer-life.

The pastor who is not praying is playing;
the people who are not praying are straying.

The two prerequisites to successful Christian living are vision and passion, both of which are born in and maintained by prayer.

The ministry of preaching is open to few;
the ministry of prayer—the highest ministry of all human offices—is open to all.

Prayer grasps eternity!

The understanding soul prays;
the praying soul gets understanding.

The secret of praying is praying in secret.

Elijah was a man skilled in the art of prayer,
who altered the course of nature,
strangled the economy of a nation,
prayed and fire fell,
prayed and people fell,
prayed and rain fell.
We need rain, rain, rain!
The churches are so parched
that seed cannot germinate.
Our altars are dry,
with no hot tears of penitents.
Oh for an Elijah!

Elijah was a man subject to like passions as we are,
but alas, we are not men of like prayer as he was.
His whole life is summed up in two words,
"He prayed" (James 5:17).

Watch and pray,
or rust and decay.

No amount of prayer will deliver us from temptation,
but it will deliver us in temptation.

Prayer is the language of the poor in Spirit.

The self-sufficient do not need to pray;
The self-satisfied will not pray;
The self-righteous cannot pray.

Prayer produces courage and joy
to do God's will
even if tears are shed doing it.

The man who kneels in prayer
has some standing before the Lord.

Many ask God for help.
Few ask God for mercy.

We need preachers who can preach up a storm, but
our greater need is for pray-ers who can pray down the fire.

Most Christians pray to be blest—few pray to be broken.

Prayer is not argument with God
to persuade Him to walk our way,
but an exercise by which He enables us by His
Spirit to walk His way.

Who can tell the measure of God's power?
Prayer is as vast as God
because He is behind it.
Prayer is as mighty as God, because He has
committed Himself to answer it.

B. Revival

"True revival," said dear Dr. Tozer, "changes the moral climate of a community." Wet-eyed, heart-broken revivalists produce wet-eyed, heart-broken sinners at the feet of a holy God.

The evangelism of the last twenty-five years has been the most costly in history. High-powered methods have needed high-powered men with high salaries to get them to function. Revival never costs a penny. It is the Lord's <u>doing</u> and is marvelous in our eyes!

This generation, rapidly sinking in a morass of materialism and swept by a blizzard of Satanic cults, can only be rescued from total loss by a heaven-sent, Sprit-born revival.

Here in the United States we live like kings compared to millions in other lands. Our greatest danger is not even moral, bad as that is, but spiritual. Prophets, as I have said and written so often, are God's emergency men for crisis hours. They thrive on perplexity, over-ride adversity, defeat calamity, bring the new wine of the Kingdom to burst the withered wineskins of orthodoxy, and birth REVIVAL. Let no Christian's heart fail him because it seems that the enemy has come in like a flood, that the voice of the prophet is not heard in the land. God has His men hidden. They will come forth <u>without price tags</u>: with nothing to sell, nothing to propagate but "holiness unto the Lord."

WHAT IS REVIVAL?
Revival is the act of the Spirit upon believers who have lost their first love.
Revival is the restoration of true doctrine.
Revival is the rekindling of the power of prayer in individuals and in groups.
Revival is seeing that God must be vindicated either by His mercy in pardoning—or by judgment!

Revival is the ascendancy of the spiritual over the material.
Revival is the Spirit's passion within the believer to know and to obey the total will of God.
Revival is the willingness to forsake all, that God might be all in all to the individual and to the Church.
Revival is the "no-time-limit" operation of God on the saints, resulting in a moving of God among the sinners.
Revival is the redeemed sobbing with broken hearts over a nation of broken lives from breaking the commandments of God.
Revival is not a luxury, but a necessity for our nation; not an alternative, but an imperative.

I am bombarded with talk or letters about the coming shortages in our national life: bread, fuel, energy. I read between the lines from people not practiced in scaring folk. They feel that the "seven years of plenty" are over for us.
The "seven years of famine" are ahead. But the greatest famine of all in the nation at this given moment is a FAMINE OF THE HEARING OF THE WORDS OF GOD (Amos 8:11).

I am sure that the main reason we do not have a national revival beginning with personal revival is that we are content to live without it.
Will the economy have to break down before God can break through and revival break out?
The discord in our disjointed society is not because of the generation gap, but because of the regeneration gap.

"They that wait upon the Lord renew their strength."
They that wait upon men usually dissipate their energies.

America could be transformed in one day if every professing Christian would live the Bible concept of Christianity for twenty-four hours. The dislocation of the status quo socially and religiously is guaranteed when spiritual revival breaks.

Apostolic purity, Apostolic piety, and Apostolic power are the need for today.

The law of revival is simply this:
   Going—weeping—bearing (seed);
   Coming—rejoicing—bringing (sheaves). (Psalms 126:6).

Can a polluted source birth a clean stream?
Can wrong men lead a nation right?
Can politicians who break divine laws establish civil laws and demand obedience to them?

John Baptist did not raise a dead person.
He did more—he raised a dead nation and a dead generation.

A proof that misery and sadness are endemic in the human race is that we need a host of comedians to try to raise a laugh.

At his expulsion from Eden, man took the wrong turn, and he has been on the wrong road ever since.

We have been spiritually satisfied with so little for so long— when there is so much land for us to possess!

Today there seem to be no recognized limits governing personal behavior. The password seems to be: do what you want, with whom you want, where you want, when you want.

If our nation has to break down materially in order that God may break through and revival break out, is the Church mature enough to welcome this?

Revival, like charity, begins at home.

Holiness teaching contradicted
by unholy living is the bane of this hour.

God's problem today is not Communism, nor yet Romanism, nor liberalism, nor modernism, nor humanism.
God's problem is dead fundamentalism!

America needs a Joan of Arc. The British need another Boadicea to wage war on her immorality. Both nations need another Jeremiah to weep over their sins, another John the Baptist to call them to repentance, and another Elijah to bring fire down from Heaven that the multitude may cry again, "The LORD, He is God! The LORD, HE is God!"

We go down to our knees, or we go down to oblivion.

We have labored in the flesh too long,
We have interpreted success by material gain—bigger buildings for our churches, bigger crowds for our hearers, bigger offerings, as proofs of His favor. We have had pygmy preachers too long. God, give us giants! We have had promoters too many. Lord, send us revivalists! We have played evangelism with a hundred gimmicks. Lord, give us, in this dark hour of human history, some John the Baptists to burn and shine, some Knox to say, "Give me Scotland (or England, or America), or I die!"

Maybe, nay, surely we need ten days in an Upper Room or maybe more suitable for us a basement to mourn the departed glory, to apologize for our arrogance in preaching so long without a NATIONAL revival.

The last revival mentioned in the Old Testament is found in the book of the prophet Joel. He proclaimed a solemn feast and said, "Let the priests, the ministers of the Lord, weep between the porch and the altar." Well, let's face it, who weeps anymore?

Before Jesus comes I am convinced that we will see a great, sweeping Pentecost that will out-Pentecost Pentecost. God will pour out His Spirit on all flesh, as Joel said. Our sons and daughters will prophesy. God will produce a race of spiritual giants for the last mighty ingathering. Today God has these leaders hidden, but in the great Day of the Lord He will bring them to light, and the last shall be first. I pray that day will come soon.

Let the Church live again with holy passion and America will be reborn. THERE IS NO OTHER DOOR OF HOPE.

God said, "I will pour out my Spirit upon all flesh. . . . BEFORE the great and terrible day of the Lord come" (Acts 2:17, 20). If it is true that greater is He that is in us than he that is in the world, and it is true; if it is true that the gates of hell shall not prevail against His Church, and it is true; then what have we to fear?

Spiritual and moral revolution is only possible to men whose "eyes have seen the glory of the coming of the Lord"!

C. Missions

Christ cared enough for sinners
to die for them.
Do we care enough for sinners
to live to reach them?

If God could turn some of us inside out,
He might send us
to turn the world upside down.

If you don't glow, don't go.
Words are cheap—action is expensive.

Hearts of stone can never bleed
for broken hearts of flesh.

A loveless heart is a greater tragedy than having sightless
eyes or a brainless head.

A man is not to be judged
by the height of his ambitions,
but by the depth of his compassions.

Advice given to a person in adversity
may be misunderstood,
but help given in a time of trouble
needs no explanation.

"Every man is an island!"
He is an entity
incapable of identical duplication or reincarnation.

Every man is an island,
a total and complete entity—
a one-of–a-kind personality.

There is a great deal of difference between building a boat
and manning a boat.
Theologians, in the main, build the boat—
evangelists man it.

It is not God's will that any should perish.
It is not man's will that he should perish.
It is not the Church's will that he should perish.
Then why should he perish?

Without God, without hope,
millions are still calling—
how appalling!

Part V. The Conclusion

A. The Second Coming

Compared with the world population, only a few people expected Christ's first coming. So it is now. The Christians expecting His appearing are few against the millions of unbelievers in the world.

The first time He came, He entered by a woman's womb.
And no one saw Him enter.
The next time He comes, "every eye shall see Him"!

The first time He came as a Lamb.
The next time He is coming as the Lion of the tribe of Judah.

The first time He came to redeem.
The next time He is coming to reign.

The first time He came to die.
The next time He is going to raise the dead!

The first time men asked,
"Where is he that is born king of the Jews?"
The next time He is coming as the King of kings!

The first time He got a crown of thorns.
The next time He will get a crown
of glory and of gold (Rev. 14:14).

The first time He came in poverty, to a stable.
The next time He is coming in power.

The first time He had an escort of angels.
The next time "He cometh with ten thousands of his saints"
(Jude 14).

The first time He came in meekness.
The next time He is coming in majesty!
<u>BE WISE</u>
 <u>BE WARNED</u>
  <u>BEWARE</u>
Let the heathen rage
and the people imagine a vain thing.
Let iniquity abound
and the love of many wax cold.
Let the seas roar
and the land be shattered by earthquakes.
Let governments continue
to dismantle the Ten Commandments.
Let the scoffers in or outside the "church"
continue to cry:
"Where is the promise of His coming,
all things continue even as they were before?"
Let the "church" continue in her worldliness.
Let hell enlarge her mouth
to swallow the multitudes.
Let Communism design more subtle devices
to enslave the world.
Let believers wallow in more carnality,
pray less fervently,
and live more worldly.
Let fat preachers parade a thin theology.
Let us now total this end mess and mass of end-time
disobedience and rebellion.

THEN REMEMBER THIS:

"God has allowed us to know the secret of His plan, and it is
this: He purposes in His sovereign will that ALL HUMAN
HISTORY SHALL BE CONSUMMATED IN CHRIST, that
everything that exists in Heaven or earth shall find its
perfection and fulfillment in Him. And here is <u>the staggering</u>

<u>thing</u>—that in all which will one day belong to Him <u>we have been promised a share</u>." (Eph. 1:9-11, J. B. Phillips).

The <u>out</u>look on the world just now is exceedingly dark.
But! The <u>up</u>look is exceedingly glorious—
The King IS coming!

These are the incentives for His coming:
   To witness, "The Gospel must first be preached to all
      nations."
   To sacrifice, "My reward is with me" (Rev. 22:12).
   To patience, "Be patient therefore, brethren, unto the
      coming of the Lord."
   To prayer, "Watch and pray."
   To holiness of life, "He that hath this hope in him purifieth
      himself."

Are you ready for His coming?

B. The Judgment

The only way to live our todays
is in our tomorrows—
with an eye on the Judgment Seat.

The Judgment Seat
will bring no honorary degrees,
just rewards for labor.

The Judge of all the earth will do right.
He cannot be corrupted,
nor can He be corrected.

Dives and Lazarus—two beggars;
One begged here—one begged hereafter.

An anchor to Paul's soul was:
"WE MUST ALL APPEAR before the judgment seat of Christ" (2 Cor. 5:10). Living with eternity's values in view took the sting out of this oncoming test. Living "right" here on earth (I do not mean just living righteously, but living after the pattern set in the Holy Word) takes care of the hereafter.

At the Judgment Seat
all our fig leaves will drop off.

C. Eternity

The mills of God grind slowly,
but they always move on time!

These are "the last days"—
how long will they last?

The preacher who hones his sermon
On the whetstone of eternity
Will lack no hearers.

How strange that men who seek eternal youth
shun "eternal life"!

Afterword

by Paul Ravenhill

Now, at the end of this book, thinking again of the author and the yearning of his heart which transcended all that words are capable of transmitting, I look at myself and I look at the church and the question comes, "Where are we?"

Perhaps this is the echo of an eternal question which has resounded in the ether of this creation ever since the words came from God's lips in the garden: "Where? ... where? ... where? ..."

This is a question which can only be answered in relation to things other than ourselves. (We cannot say, "I am with myself." We must say, "I am behind the house," or "I am under the oak tree," etc.) Where are we with regard to the kingdom of God? What are we "behind" or "before" or "within" or "without" or "above" or "below"?

My father used to quote, "Beyond the sacred page, I seek Thee, Lord; my spirit pants for Thee, Thou Living Word." We live in an age which, like the Greeks, seems to have exalted reason and devalued everything which has to do with the more important inner aspects of being. In doing this we have cast down that which has to do with the true essence of spiritual life. It is not so much that we have become worshipers of the Word as that we have taken the Word of God as if it were a painter's palette—a base from which we mix and match our own concepts without discerning the true nature of the Spirit speaking the words. We have the words about the Spirit and think that we have the Spirit, and yet we only possess the death of words. The written word has become a substitute for the word spoken by the Spirit, the "Logos" for the "Rhema," with the result that we, as the Jews before us, have become slaves to our interpretations, bound by our own concepts and imprisoned in the darkness of our own fallen understanding.

Paul says, "If any man be in Christ he is a new creature." What does it mean to be "in" Christ? It certainly does not mean that we can be "in" (or "into" as we like to say nowadays) other things at the same time. We can only be in one place at one time—is this too difficult for us to understand? We live in the place of our hearts, not in the place of our minds, and in the place of our feelings, not the place of our religious theory. Solomon had all the theory—he had inherited all the psalms of cry and prayer and worship from his father. He systematized all of his knowledge into his three thousand proverbs and taught with a stunning exactitude, and yet died with "his heart far from God." Do we see him displayed for our example? Does it make us tremble? Does it humble us? Sometimes it seems today that we have "out-Solomoned Solomon" in our trying to understand and explain God.

Geographically speaking we can only come to a true understanding of where we are in this world in the measure in which we have become acquainted with other places, races and cultures. Spiritually speaking God must expose us to a full gamut of experience if we are to really know the place in which He would have us to dwell. We cannot see the light unless our eyes have beheld the darkness. We can only see the light of God to the degree that we have met the horrific depths of that darkness which is a foretaste of death and the dwelling place of the unclean powers of a satanic empire. Only as our souls have felt the crushing powers of evil which move over the face of the nations to rob, to kill and to destroy, can we reach forth to the power of His Resurrection.

The trouble with our age is that it wants light without having known darkness, happiness without having known pain. We live in a generation which wants only the positive and never the negative—healing without hurt, salvation without damnation, hope without despair, power without weakness, maturity without aging, knowledge without the price of learning, fullness without emptiness, joy without sorrow. The Gospel has been turned upside down as we have become conditioned to possess the kingdom without poverty of spirit, to possess comfort without mourning, and to possess the earth without paying the price of meekness.

Our problem today is that we have tried to make it all too easy. We have done with the Word as the ants do in their storing of seeds; we have filled the germ so that we might keep the seed sterile without the inconvenience of having it shoot forth in growth to upset our plans. We have avoided the hurt and pain and loss and invented a "contemporary" (cursed word) Christian culture. God won't have it and so we are left, as the people in Isaiah, to wither "by the hand of our iniquities." Our mental games will not hold up in exposure to reality, and in choosing the theory of a man-engendered Christianity we find that we have chosen death. This is not a static state but rather a kingdom of falsehood which drags us down into an ever-deepening morass as we struggle to build for ourselves and for our contemporaries God's true house on a shattered foundation.

Only as we return to the presence of the living God can we hope to find reality. In the beginning was Reality, before there was anything false or evil. I believe God's call for us is to go beyond the physical world, beyond the world of man's thoughts and fears and imagination. We are called to Reality, beyond all the sham and shame and sickness and sin which the enemy has built up around mankind and around the church. We are called to live and breathe, to abide and to walk in the realm of the life of the Spirit of God.

I believe the day is coming, and now is, when God will start to call forth a people formed in the mold of the original purpose of God—a people who have tasted the joy of that kingdom which is not of earth, and have counted all else but dross. "We" can never fight and overcome the earthly—we are the earthly. Liberation and transformation, the heart of the Gospel message, are possible only as the kingdom of God in its true spiritual essence takes root in our lives and springs up overwhelming every other presence, every other influence.

I believe that there is a principle involved when Jesus says to Peter, "Upon this rock I will build. . ." Peter has seen and declared Jesus to be the Son of the Living God and, in effect, Jesus is saying, "Peter, everything you have seen in Me I give to you. . . You see

Me with the keys of heaven and earth, you see Me with the power to bind and loose—Peter, the keys and the power which you see in Me I give to you. As you see me and My power, your portion will be to share in My kingdom and to participate in the outworking of its power."

Perhaps we have been taught too much to look upon the negative in all our looking at the Bible. We have stood with Adam as he fell and lost a kingdom and inherited a curse as judgment, but we have never seen or stood with Adam in the glorious majesty and victory of the day when he stood before God and all created beings, and in total dominion could answer God's question, "What is this?" We have not seen him, I say, when he stood, and discerning the heart of God he discerned the nature and named the name, one after another, of every living creature that walked the face of this whole vast earth. We have not thrilled with his triumph, nor felt the call of God in our own spirits to discern and to name every part of the whole nature of our own world.

We have read of Noah, but do we feel the immensity of the pathos of the world-ending judgment and the overwhelming glory of the resurrection purpose of God locked in his breast and paid for in his life throughout one hundred and twenty years? We read of Moses and of David and the prophets, but have we ever heard the question within ourselves, "understandest thou what thou readest," shocking us into living awareness?

Some day we will stand before God, and before the Word of God, and in that moment we will see all as it really is in the clear light of eternity. The power and the passion of the world to come will be absolutely clear to us then, in that morning without clouds. Yet God is the same today; His will and His purpose will not be any different then from what they are now. Maybe the land is yet "afar off," but His call to us, and His Spirit's call through us, is ever for the fulfillment—"Thy kingdom come. . ." There is nothing more glorious for this old earth, nor is there for the child of God, than the attaining to the Presence of the One Who reigneth for ever and ever and being a living part of His Kingdom.

Torch My Heart

Lord engage my heart today
With zeal that will not pass away.
Now torch it with Thy holy fire
That never more shall time's desire
Invade or quench the Heaven-born power.
I would be trapped within Thy holy will,
Thine every holy purpose to fulfill
That every effort of my life shall bring
Rapturous praise to my Eternal King.
I pledge from this day to the grave
To be Thine own unquestioning slave.
                    —Leonard Ravenhill

(The last poem written by Leonard Ravenhill at 2:30 a.m. on February 12, 1994, nine months before he "passed into life.")

Lightning Source UK Ltd.
Milton Keynes UK
UKHW010239230121
377534UK00001B/31